THE RUCK

by Kevin Fegan

Published by Playdead Press 2017

© Kevin Fegan 2017

Kevin Fegan has asserted his rights under the Copyright, Design and Patents Act, 1988, to be identified as the author of this work.

A CIP catalogue record for this book is available from the British Library.

ISBN 978-1-910067-55-0

Caution
All rights whatsoever in this play are strictly reserved and application for performance should be sought through the author before rehearsals begin. No performance may be given unless a license has been obtained.

This book is sold subject to the condition that it shall not by way of trade or otherwise, be lent, resold, hired out, or otherwise circulated without the publisher's prior consent in any form of binding or cover other than that in which it is published and without a similar condition including this condition being imposed on the subsequent purchaser.

Playdead Press
www.playdeadpress.com

The Ruck by Kevin Fegan was co-produced by Creative Scene and the Lawrence Batley Theatre. It was first performed at Lawrence Batley Theatre, Huddersfield, on 15th & 16th Sept 2017, followed by a short tour of Yorkshire theatres. The play was commissioned by Creative Scene, funded by The Arts Council England.

CAST

Josie Cerise	Emley
Emma Ashton	Nan/Hazel
Esther-Grace Button	Shelley
Richard Hand	Spen
Sophie Mercer	Iffy
Sam Winterbottom	Calder
Emily Spowage	Heaton
Robert Took	Kiwi Pete/Uncle Logan

Special thanks to Jon Adamson who was unfortunately injured during rehearsals and had to drop out of the cast.

CREATIVE TEAM

Director	Joyce Branagh
Writer	Kevin Fegan
Designer	Olivia du Monceau
Producer	Rose Cuthbertson
Assistant Director	Rebecca Foster
Composer/MD	Rebekah Hughes
Choreographer	Rachel Gee
Lighting Designer	Chris Brearley
Stage Manager	Jessica Thanki-Grogan
Technical Stage Manager	Jonathan Hudson

For Lawrence Batley Theatre:

Director	Victoria Firth
Production Manager	Rupert Horder
Marketing Manager	Laura Rodwell

For Creative Scene:

Executive Producer	Vicky Holliday
Marketing Officer	Lisa Slattery
Project Manager	Rosie Clarke
Press Officer	Alison Bellamy

Special Thanks to Craig Taylor, Batley Bulldogs Women's and Girls' teams Coach, and the team players of Batley Bulldogs Under 16's Girls' Team 2015.

Thanks also to the families and friends of the girls' team who have helped to inspire this show; to Batley Bulldogs Rugby League Club, especially Paul Harrison, and to Proper Job Theatre Company for Kevin's residency at the club and early script development.

In Australia, thanks to Dave McCall, Rugby League Coach at Merrimac State high School and to Mel and Amanda Steadman.

FOREWORD

by Nancy Barrett, Director at Creative Scene.

'The Ruck' grew out of a residency first undertaken by Proper Job Theatre Company and writer Kevin Fegan at Batley Bulldogs Rugby League Club in 2015. In this part of Yorkshire, Rugby League rules and Batley Bulldogs is a team that's been battling from its famously raked pitch on Mount Pleasant since 1880 – a mile or so from the centre of this former textile town. So we knew there was a rich seam of stories to mine as local theatre company, Proper Job, began work with the Club and brought Kevin in to explore some of the stories. The sport, the town and the community around the club have all changed dramatically and writer Kev found that it was the Under 16's girls' team that was drawing him to tell their story. This is a story of sporting achievement with a difference. It is inspired by the journey of U.K. Champions, the mighty Batley Girls U16 team, from the original "County of Origin" of Rugby League Football, as they travel to the Gold Coast on their historic tour of Queensland, Australia - the first British girls' team to do so. These girls are growing up together and are used to challenges, both on and off the pitch; but are they prepared for what's in store?

The play has a very 'northern' feel, with a flavour of working class variety performance and universal themes of coming of age, family relationships and friendships, told against the history and traditions of Rugby League and changes in society. Creative Scene is pleased to have commissioned this new play and brought it into production with Lawrence Batley Theatre.

Creative Scene is Arts Council England's Creative People and Places project in West Yorkshire. We aim to make art a part of everyday life in the areas where people are less likely to get involved in arts and cultural activities.

We want to make a lasting change in the way people take part in, make and experience the arts, to generate an appetite and sustain a programme into the future through new co-commissioning and co-producing partnerships, increased local delivery and fundraising capacity, and securing continued investment into the area. To do this, we commission, produce and programme a wide range of events from touring theatre in pubs to large scale outdoor arts in parks and towns centre.

We work with festivals, museums, parks, businesses, community, sports, and social clubs, to engage new audiences, find accessible spaces to present work, and to unearth the stories that resonate with contemporary urban communities.

Creative Scene is developed and managed through a consortium led by The Lawrence Batley Theatre, The Batley Festival Group, and Kirklees Council.

www.creativescene.org.uk
www.thelbt.org

Kevin Fegan is a Playwright & Poet. Kevin has written to commission over fifty original plays for a wide variety of theatre. He has four new stage plays in production in September 2017 including "The Shed Crew" (Red Ladder), "Down The Line" (Barrow Hill Roundhouse Railway Centre featuring "The Flying Scotsman") and "Bess - the Commoner Queen" (The Guildhall Theatre Derby).

Recent work includes "Obama the Mamba", Curve and The Lowry (Nominated Best New Play Manchester Theatre Awards 2012). Also for The Lowry: "Slave", Feelgood Theatre 2010, followed by national tour (Winner Pete Postlethwaite Best New Play Manchester Theatre Awards 2010 and Winner Best Play or Film Human Trafficking Foundation 2011); "Fireflies: a love story waiting to happen" (nominated Best New Play Manchester Evening News Theatre Awards 2010); "The Forest" (2008) and adaptations of "Love on the Dole" (nominated Best Special Entertainment M.E.N. Theatre Awards 2004) and "Oh Wot A Lovely War" (2006). Early stage plays for Contact Theatre Manchester include "McAlpine's Fusilier"1988 (nominated Best New Play M.E.N Theatre Awards); "Excess XS" (Winner Best New Play in UK Regions Plays International 1992) and "Strange Attractors: love in a virtual world ", in collaboration with Granada TV (Winner Best New Play in UK Regions Plays International 1994); "Private Times" for The Library Theatre Manchester (nominated Best New Play M.E.N. Theatre Awards 1990) & in 1999 performed by prisoners and staff at H.M.Prison Grendon; "Rule 43" (Cracked Actors British prisons tour 1989 & 90, nominated Best New Play M.E.N. Theatre Awards 1989) and a community play for Moss Side/Hulme in 1993 "Game Challenge Level 7" (N.I.A.Centre & Contact Theatre). Large-scale site-specific work includes "Lord Dynamite" (co-written with John Fox), a Welfare State International production for L.I.F.T.'91; "The Clay Man" at Upper Campfield Market Manchester (a Manchester City of Drama 1994 production and Woolaton Park Nottingham); "Seven-Tenths" for Walk the Plank Theatre Ship (British tour by sea, nominated Best Special Entertainment M.E.N. Theatre Awards 1996); "52 Degrees South"(co-written & co-directed with Andy Farrell) at the Imperial War Museum North (Winner of Best New Play M.E.N. Theatre Awards 2002; "Captured Live" (Leicester Haymarket Theatre 2004) and "Not Much Matches Mansfield" (Mansfield Palace Theatre 2013). Devised work includes Quarantine's award-winning White Trash" (Contact Theatre 2004) and "EatEat" (Leicester Haymarket Theatre 2003). Plays for young people include "Get Real" (Blackpool Grand Theatre 2003); "The Ghosts of Crime Lake" (Oldham Coliseum Theatre 2005); "When Frankenstein Came to Matlock" (Mansfield Palace Theatre 2008); "ABC123" and "The Selkie Boy" (Ashton Group at Forum 28 Theatre Barrow 2009 & 2010) and "Wan2tlk?" (Liverpool Everyman Theatre 2001 and published by Methuen Drama 2008). Kevin has written several single plays for BBC Radio 4, plus a Classic Serial and a Woman's Hour serial. "Blast" was nominated for a Best Drama Sony Award 2001 and the stage version at Contact was a Manchester Poetry Festival Airport Commission in 2002. He has written a few short films, including "Dancing in The Ruins" (in collaboration with Granada TV). He has also worked as a storyline writer for Granada TV's "Coronation St". Kevin has published 10 books of poetry and edited over a dozen anthologies and is a regular performer of his own work.

www.kevinfegan.co.uk

THE RUCK
by Kevin Fegan

CAST OF 8

5F | 3M

CHARACTERS

SHELLEY | team player for Batley Girls' Rugby League Club.

EMLEY | team player for Batley Girls.

HEATON | team player for Batley Girls.

IFFY | Muslim Asian Girl and latest recruit to Batley Girls.

SPEN | Team Coach for Batley Girls and Shelley's Dad

NAN | Heaton's Grandma

KIWI PETE | Emley's Dad

CALDER | Emley's Boyfriend and friend of Iffy.

UNCLE LOGAN | Heaton's Australian "uncle".

HAZEL | Australian Team Coach for Smiley High State School

CHORUS and all other parts are played by the cast

Suggestions for doubling

NAN / HAZEL

KIWI PETE / UNCLE LOGAN

RAPS & SONGS

LIFE IS A RUCK

JIHADI RAP

HERITAGE ROAD

KICK IT INTO TOUCH

PARENTS & TEENAGERS

PROLOGUE: "COUNTY OF ORIGIN"

A training session with Batley Girls Rugby League Football Club. The girls (Shelley, Emley and Heaton) are warming up with coach, Spen, before the session starts. The other members of the cast are watching the girls training.

CHORUS: From the boundary of Mount Pleasant,
looking out across the valley,
lies a classic sweep of northern industrial archaeology.
This settlement, called Batley,
is carved from brutal rock.
The blackened brick
of Victorian viaducts and rolling mills
defines the shape of our society.
There was a time these valleys
were the playground of kings
who claimed their sport was ordained by God,
until their power was tackled by noblemen
in battle after bloody battle.
In time, the birthright of the aristocracy
was snatched from them by the industrialists
who easily out-paced them with their power of money
and went on to score a lasting victory.
But then the working man created a ruck
and with his labour forced the bourgeoisie
to share their wealth and settle for democracy.
Finally, in these epic Heartlands,
Woman wrestled free from the rib-cage of Man

to take her place in the arena and stake
her claim in the game we call society.
There are those who would turn back the clock,
but the genie is out of the box,
the sport can never be the same again.
There have been too many game-changers;
but, wait, here comes the latest stranger
to take the stage, determined to play the
Northern Game.

SCENE ONE

Iffy, a 16 year old Asian girl, and the team's latest recruit, steps forward to join the girls.

EMLEY: Wedding reception's upstairs.

IFFY: I'm not here for a wedding.

SHELLEY: Cricket pitch is over there.

IFFY: Very funny.

SPEN: This is our new girl, Ifra. Apparently it means "to fix and improve something".

EMLEY: She can't play rugby.

IFFY: Why not?

EMLEY: Because Asians don't play rugby.

SPEN: This one does.

IFFY: Frightened we'll take over the rugby – like we did the cricket?

EMLEY: That's not going to happen on my watch.

IFFY: I mean, we've moved into drugs and organised crime, why not rugby?

EMLEY: She can't play rugby in a headscarf.

IFFY: It's an hijab.

SPEN: Right, you know the drill. "Touch and Pass" around the field until you find out five things about the new girl.

GIRLS:	(*chanting while they run with the ball*) Touch and pass, kick some ass, whatever it takes, they will not pass. Making contact keeps us strong touch our hearts and pass it on.
EMLEY:	Where you from?
IFFY:	Heritage Road.
EMLEY:	No, I mean "originally"?
IFFY:	Duh, Batley – born and bred. I know what you meant. Grandad came here from Pakistan without a penny in his pocket to work in textiles. My dad went on to own the mill. He turned it into a furniture warehouse when textiles went down the toilet.
GIRLS:	Touch and pass, kick some ass, whatever it takes, they will not pass. Making contact keeps us strong touch our hearts and pass it on.
SHELLEY:	So this is you trying to make a name for yourself, is it? Playing rugby?
IFFY:	Why not?
SHELLEY:	What position?
IFFY:	Scrum half - I like to boss it.
GIRLS:	Touch and pass, kick some ass, whatever it takes, they will not pass.

	Making contact keeps us strong touch our hearts and pass it on.
IFFY:	(*to Emley*) Why do you play? You strike me as a bit of a "girly girl".
EMLEY:	I am not.
IFFY:	You're wearing make-up for training.
EMLEY:	Foundation is not make-up.
SHELLEY:	Slapper.
IFFY:	I suppose you never know who's watching, do you?
SHELLEY:	Yeah, we get loads of modelling scouts at the rugby.
EMLEY:	Shurrup lesbo!
SHELLEY:	Tart!
SPEN:	(*calling*) Hey! You never heard your father using language like that!
IFFY:	Is Coach Spen your dad?
SHELLEY:	Yeah.
IFFY:	Bet he started this team for you, didn't he?
SHELLEY:	No.
GIRLS:	Touch and pass, kick some ass, whatever it takes, they will not pass. Making contact keeps us strong

	touch our hearts and pass it on.
IFFY:	Who's the quiet one?
SHELLEY:	Heaton – we call her "Hanging Heaton" –
EMLEY:	'Cos she's morbid.
SHELLEY:	She's a good Prop Forward.
IFFY:	(*to Heaton*) Why do you play?
EMLEY:	She enjoys the bruises.
HEATON:	So what if I do? They're badges of honour.
IFFY:	Bet you let your anger out on the pitch, don't you?
EMLEY:	Like when you head-butted that Wigan Full Back.
HEATON:	She fell onto me.
EMLEY:	Yeah, right.
SHELLEY:	She was defending me.
GIRLS:	Touch and pass, kick some ass, whatever it takes, they will not pass. Making contact keeps us strong touch our hearts and pass it on.
EMLEY:	(*calling*) Ready, Coach!
SHELLEY:	We've only found out four things about the new girl.
SPEN:	It'll have to do.

The Girls return to Spen.

"THE RUCK"

SPEN: Life is a ruck
But you make your own luck in this world.
Enjoy the battle,
Go in hard on the tackle,
Turn defence into attack.
So what if life sucks?
Who gives a flying... Prop Forward?
Be a play-maker,
Not an undertaker.
Make like a Hooker
Cashing in on a scrum,
On a dummy run;
Where there's muck, there's money,
Make a fast buck,
Look for those opportunities,
You gotta be duckin' and divin'
Or you'll come unstuck.
Not everyone's a crook,
So don't play the victim,
Don't swallow the rhetoric,
Hook, line and sinker.
Have no truck with defeat,
Pluck up the courage,
If you're in at the deep end,
Down on your luck,
Last line of defence,
Take aim,
Right pass at the right time,
Swing it out to a safe pair of hands,

Running with the ball, down the wing
Towards the goal line
And try! Try again!

Iffy steps up and places the ball for a kick at goal. Emley steps up to take it as usual but coach Spen indicates he would like Iffy to have a go. Emley is not best pleased. Iffy kicks a goal. They all congratulate her, except Emley.

SPEN: I think we've found ourselves a new kicker!

EMLEY: (*to Iffy*) What you really doing here?

Iffy launches into her "JIHADI RAP"

IFFY: What's a matter, girl,
Am I upsetting your view of the world?
Worried I'm some kind of infiltrator?
A spy in the camp? A people-hater?
Well, let me tell you this:
We're not all "Jihadi brides", me and my sisters,
On a one-way ticket to Syria, off to join I.S.I.S.
Yeah, I'm on a mission,
But look - no bombs,
We're in this together,
Who gives a shit where you're from?
Batley's not Jihad,
More like rehab,
Like a broken Fox's biscuit,
It's up to us to fix it,
There'll be no game left to play
If you and me can't mix it.

EMLEY: Muslim!

IFFY: Kafir!

EMLEY: What's that?

IFFY: Non-believer.

SHELLEY: Is that bad?

IFFY: Depends.

SHELLEY: Are there any good Kafirs?

IFFY: Some. Are there any good Muslims?

SHELLEY: There could be you?

I'm Shelley.

HEATON: Heaton.

EMLEY: (*begrudgingly*) Emley.

SHELLEY: Do you want to hang out with us, after, at Tescos?

IFFY: There's something else about me you should know: you might be the present, but I'm the future. So that's five things you know about me now.

SPEN: Right ladies, listen up, I've got some big news for you. I know we're U.K. Champions – no one can take that away from us; but, truth is, only one or two clubs have ever been a match for us. You girls are good, don't get me wrong, but we're not used to playing teams who are more than a match for us. That is, until we faced those Ozzie girls at the end of the season. They taught us our biggest lesson of last year: that we can be beaten. I know we could've beat them, but the fact is we didn't.

HEATON: They were tough: they went swimming in the sea at Whitby in Winter.

SPEN: Beating teams who are better than us, that's our real challenge. The standard of competition in Australia is obviously higher; which is why I've been talking to your parents about going to Queensland on a pre-season tour.

EMLEY: Queensland? Where's that?

HEATON: Australia, stupid.

EMLEY: What? Us? Going to Australia? We can't do that?

SPEN: If those Ozzie girls can tour the U.K., why can't we tour Australia?

HEATON: My Nan won't be able to afford it.

SPEN: For a while now we've been busy fund-raising up at Soothill Working Mens' Club. We didn't want to say until we were confident we could afford to take the whole team. Those who can afford to pay are paying, those who can't will be subsidised; so I don't want girls worrying about the money. We're still ten grand short, but with your help, I think we can do it. I've been in touch with their Coach, Hazel, and she's happy to host us for a pre-season tour. We'll be staying on the Gold Coast, in a hotel, and travelling around Queensland, playing some of their top teams. Any questions?

EMLEY: Is there a beach?

SPEN: It's called the "Gold Coast" – what do you think?

EMLEY: I think I need a new bikini.

SHELLEY: Can we train on the beach?

SPEN: Every morning. The hotel's walking distance to the beach.

HEATON: When are we going?

SPEN: End of October – for three weeks. It's the start of their Summer so it'll be hot – which is another advantage they'll have over us, if we're not super fit.

SHELLEY: What about school?

SPEN: We're going over half-term, but you will miss a week of school.

EMLEY: Yes!

SPEN: Hey, you lot, listen up: I've had to fight hard for this. I've promised your teachers you'll catch up on your work. I expect you all to do

	as well in your exams as in your rugby. Treat your brain like a muscle and exercise it.
SHELLEY:	She'll have to find hers first.
EMLEY:	Look who's talking.
SPEN:	Pack up your kit and get some rest. Training three times a week from now on, until Oz.
IFFY:	Spen, am I going?
SPEN:	You're in the team, aren't you?

Girls collect their bags to leave. Spen calls back Heaton for a word.

SPEN:	I don't want you worrying about the money, okay?
HEATON:	Thanks, Coach.
SPEN:	Let me see your arms.

She shows him.

HEATON:	They're healing.
SPEN:	Good girl. I told you the rugby would help. Off you go.

SCENE TWO

Spen is outside Batley Bulldogs' stadium on Heritage Road, looking down at the surrounding area of Mount Pleasant.

SPEN: It were wool 'round here, cotton in Lancashire. The "shoddy trade", they called it: woollen rags and clothes recycled into blankets, carpets and military uniforms. There were some very wealthy "shoddy barons" made their money on the sweat of others. They still call the League 'round here, the "Heavy Woollen". Mount Pleasant was a temperance area because of the Methodist influence. I suppose the Muslim community are continuing that tradition. But Batley has always been a heavy-drinking town. Still is, especially at weekends along the "golden mile". It were Batley Variety Club what put the town on the map, with international superstars like Louis Armstrong, Eartha Kitt, Cliff Richards, The Bee Gees, Roy Orbison... the list goes on.

I have a theory that all the sweat from the mills gave rise to Rugby League. You see, hard labour, well, it builds a man up, physically, like a warrior. Mix that with a sense of social injustice and you've got one very aggressive and righteous individual. And all that aggression has to go somewhere. Best not twat your boss; better to find yourself an arena and charge like a bull at another bloke built like a brick shithouse. In times of war, throw a weapon into the equation and you've got yourself a soldier. In peace-time, throw a ball in there and you've got a rugby league player. That's why it was created here, in Kirklees, down the road at the George Hotel in 1895. This is the "County of Origin". The following year, Batley were the very first winners of the Northern Union Challenge Cup – "Champions of the North" they called us. Those were the days, when the town's brass band would turn out for the team and the railways would sound a salute. I remember my dad bringing me here, standing me under his crombie to keep warm. His dad used to take him when there were anti-aircraft guns on the hills opposite.

Me dad says,

"You knew where you were in those days. Rugby Union for the toffs and Rugby League for the roughs." Of course, now you've working-class kids like me been to university and playing Rugby Union as well as League.

Dad says,

"They had the money, but we were faster, more physical and they used to come to us for the best coaches. Players would work a twelve-hour shift, then come straight to a match to play. You could tell a player by how they ran or threw a ball. You never knew what might emerge from a scrum. They used to score tries from 80 yards out. Wingers would play wide like Wingers. Nowadays it's driven by possession and the six-tackle rule. They just seem to get down for a rest in a scrum."

It's a different game since Super League. Much harder for us little clubs to compete against the big money-teams. It's not a level playing field. Mind you, it never was at The Mount, with our infamous slope down to the "Nine 'Ole". Training is fierce for these full-time professionals. I reckon the players are getting bigger and fitter, but the body contact takes its toll and leads to more injuries.

This area, where the Club is, on Mount Pleasant around Heritage Road, used to be a white working-class area. Players used to live local and play local. The community used to turn out for the home games. We used to belong here. Now one ghetto's been swopped for another: we're surrounded by mosques and madrasses. I've nothing against the Muslim community, but they're not interested in rugby, are they? Apart from Iffy, of course. I don't know what's going on there.

On match days the ground still comes to life, but the rest of the time the Club looks like the museum on the hill. And "The Taverners", next to the ground, where we all used to meet for a few pints, well, supporters stopped going 'cause they don't live 'round here no more. It was taken over by Asian businessmen and, well, it's burned down now. What can we do? We can't turn the clocks back. We can't move the stadium. I don't know what the future has in store.

SONG: "HERITAGE ROAD"

SPEN / CHORUS: The future grows, the past erodes,
History uploads on Heritage Road.
The people sweat and the people play,
In the rolling valleys of green and grey,
Migrant workers come and go,
Communities change but the landscape don't.
The time has come, mills and mines all gone,
We must adapt our lives and try to move on.

Changes to work, changes to play,
In the rolling valleys of green and grey.
As the future grows and the past erodes,
History uploads on Heritage Road.
Looking back at all we've done,
Goods produced and tournaments won,
We face the challenge of a brand new day
In the rolling valleys of green and grey.
The future grows and the past erodes,
History uploads on Heritage Road.

SCENE THREE

The Girls are gathering outside Tescos in Batley.

SHELLEY: Coach says we have to think up a name for the team.

EMLEY: We've got a name - Batley Girls.

SHELLEY: No, stupid, a nickname. Like the men are "Bulldogs".

IFFY: What? Like "Batley Poodles"?

EMLEY: Can we be "Batley Labradoodles"?

SHELLEY: This is serious. We have to sex it up –

HEATON: (*to Emley*) That's your department –

SHELLEY: Like Kerry Packer did when he got the clubs to choose animal names.

HEATON: Does it have to be an animal?

SHELLEY: No, there's "Huddersfield Giants" and -

HEATON: We could be insects -

EMLEY: "Batley Bumble Bees".

HEATON: Or vegetables –

EMLEY: "Batley Brussels".

IFFY: Birds?

EMLEY: "Batley Blackbirds".

IFFY: Cheap gag.

HEATON: "Batley Dinosaurs".

SHELLEY: Go on, take the piss; see how you feel when the new kit arrives.

EMLEY: You never said we were getting a new strip?

SHELLEY: Well, we are. When we choose a name. We've got ourselves a sponsor for Oz.

HEATON: Who?

SHELLEY: Morley Waste.

EMLEY: Oh, great, we're gonna be "Batley Dustbins".

SHELLEY: They've said we can suggest something. Otherwise, it will be their choice.

Calder arrives with a couple of mates (played by Kiwi Pete, Spen and Nan). There is a stand-off between the girl and the boys.

IFFY: I know that boy.

EMLEY: You do?

IFFY: Yeah, Calder, he used to live on our street before all the white boys left.

EMLEY: He's my boyfriend.

IFFY: Oh, sorry, I didn't mean to –

EMLEY: That's all right, it's nothing serious; he's just some boy.

GIRLS CHORUS: Things girls like about boys:

      they're funny
      they're not so bothered about their appearance
      not as bitchy as girls
      make you feel protected
      nice bums
      show their feelings when they're on their own
      have ideas and thoughts about things
      a shoulder to cry on.

BOYS CHORUS: Things boys like about girls:
      hair and eyes
      they have the babies
      do things boys don't want to do - like cleaning
      they're more caring
      put a lot of effort into their appearance
      make us feel happy and horny
      they smile
      you can talk to them about personal shit.

CALDER: Someone got shot here.

EMLEY: Yeah, we heard.

CALDER: You shouldn't be hanging 'round Tescos.

IFFY: It wasn't here, it was down near the garage.

CALDER: And you would know.

EMLEY: What's that supposed to mean?

CALDER: This is not a place for girls.

SHELLEY: This is not a place for boys.

GIRLS CHORUS: Things girls don't like about boys:
     can get obsessed with you
     show off in front of their mates
     send you dirty pictures on Instagram
     ignore you and insensitive
     immature and big-headed
     don't listen and selfish attitudes
     jealous and they have affairs
     too loud and sexist.

BOYS CHORUS: Things boys don't like about girls:
     gossiping and constant nagging
     too much perfume and too pink
     go to the toilet in pairs
     drag us into town shopping
     take too long getting ready
     they don't answer your texts
     can't understand them and too emotional
     expect us to be mind readers.

Girls mimic the boys' postures and attitudes.

Boys mimic the girls' postures and attitudes.

GIRLS CHORUS: "Get your tits out for the lads!"

BOYS CHORUS: "Does my bum look big in this?"

GIRLS CHORUS: "If you really loved me, you'd let me."

BOYS CHORUS: "Haven't you had enough to drink yet?"

GIRLS CHORUS: "Yeah, I've done it loads of times."

BOYS CHORUS: "I want you to want to."

GIRLS CHORUS: "Can we go out with each other and still see other people?"

BOYS CHORUS: "Were you staring at her?"

GIRLS CHORUS: "You decide for us."

BOYS CHORUS: "Sorry isn't good enough."

GIRLS CHORUS: "Bitch, ho, bird, chick, the wife!"

BOYS CHORUS: "Huh, men!"

Shelley and Emley stick together. Iffy goes over to Calder.

IFFY: Emley's very pretty.

CALDER: Do you think so?

IFFY: Well, you obviously do.

CALDER: She's not like you.

IFFY: What do you mean?

CALDER: Nothing.

IFFY: No, come on? You mean, Asian?

CALDER: No! I mean she wears lots of make-up.

IFFY: And?

CALDER: And perfume. We were in the cinema the other night and I could hardly breathe. I was choking on the stink, it was that bad.

IFFY: Tell her.

CALDER: I don't want to hurt her feelings. And she's got sharp nails.

IFFY: That is more information than I need to know.

CALDER: Come out with us tomorrow night?

IFFY: I'm not playing gooseberry.

CALDER: Don't be daft, it'll be a laugh.

IFFY: Not for Emley, it won't.

CALDER: Come on, we used to have a right laugh together.

IFFY: Yeah, we did. Now go and see your girlfriend, Calder; you're doin' my head in.

Iffy joins Shelley and Emley joins Calder.

EMLEY: (*to Calder*) Let's find somewhere private we can make out.

SHELLEY: (*to Iffy*) So what about this name?

SCENE FOUR

Heaton's house.

HEATON: Did you know about this tour, Nan?

NAN: I've told Spen we can't afford it.

HEATON: We don't have to, he's raising the money.

NAN: We're not a charity case.

HEATON: Dunt stop you using the Food Bank.

NAN: That's different. You don't want to be going to Australia.

HEATON: Can you let me decide what I want?

NAN: No good'll come of it.

HEATON: Just cos it didn't work out for you and grandad. I'm not migrating, you know; I am coming back.

NAN: We came back so you could have a decent life here.

HEATON: What? In Batley? With an alcoholic mother.

NAN: We didn't know how things would turn out.

HEATON: I'm going and you can't stop me.

Heaton goes to her room and waits by her laptop for a face-time call. On screen we see a video call come through, which she answers and Logan appears on screen.

LOGAN: Is that you, Heaton?

HEATON: Uncle Logan?

LOGAN: Too right it is. Good to see you, girl, finally.

HEATON: Good to see you too.

LOGAN: So you're the rugby player?

HEATON: Yeah.

LOGAN: Cool. I'll have to come and see you play.

HEATON: Really?

LOGAN: If you're coming all the way to Queensland, we'll have to meet up.

HEATON: I'd love that.

LOGAN: No dramas. We love our rugby league over here.

HEATON: My friends'll be dead jealous.

LOGAN: We can work on that if you want. I'll show you a few places to make your friends turn green.

HEATON: I can't wait to meet you.

LOGAN: You really look like your mother when you say that.

HEATON: Do I?

LOGAN: How is she?

HEATON: In a bad way. Don't you know?

LOGAN: You're the first one in the family to get in touch.

HEATON: We don't see much of her, she's too busy drinking herself to death.

LOGAN: Sorry to hear that. I was always very fond of your mother.

HEATON: I've never heard anyone say that before.

LOGAN: You said you live with your Gran?

HEATON: Since mum lost the plot.

LOGAN: What about your grandad – he's my uncle?

HEATON: He left Nan, not long after they all came back from Oz; but I was just a baby so I'm not sure.

LOGAN: Sounds like you guys have had it pretty tough.

HEATON: Do you remember them?

LOGAN: Sure do.

Heaton hears her Nan approaching.

HEATON: Shit! Nan's coming. Sorry, I've got to go, I'll be in touch soon.

Heaton ends the call. Nan enters.

NAN: Look, we should talk about this.

HEATON: Do we have any relatives in Queensland?

NAN:	We don't have anything to do with your grandad's side of the family.
HEATON:	Why not?
NAN:	They're a bad lot; you keep away.
HEATON:	What about "Uncle" Logan?
NAN:	Who told you about – ?
HEATON:	I found him myself, online.
NAN:	What have I told you about talking to strangers on the internet?
HEATON:	He's not really my uncle; he's mum's cousin.
NAN:	I know who he is.
HEATON:	What's your problem? Do you think he's "grooming" me?
NAN:	Don't joke about things you know nothing about.
HEATON:	Yeah, cos no one tells me fuck-all.
NAN:	Language!

Heaton storms out.

SONG: "KICK IT INTO TOUCH"

HEATON: I don't want to be the next big thing,
I don't want to end up like my mum,
I don't want to meet no pervy celebrities,
I don't want a Staffie called Tyson.

I don't want millions of followers and friends
or drink myself stupid, living for the weekends.
I don't really care what's #trending
or the latest hits YouTube are recommending.
Constantly broke,
and I've no phone credit,
life is one big joke
and I just don't get it.
I need to kick it into touch!

CHORUS: Constantly broke,
up to our necks in credit,
life is one big joke
and we just don't get it.
Kick it into touch!

HEATON: I don't want to have no superpowers
or be a vampire zombie head,
I don't want to star in a brat movie,
and I don't want to talk to the dead.
Constantly broke,
and no phone credit,
life is one big joke
and I just don't get it.
I need to kick it into touch!

CHORUS: Constantly broke,
up to our necks in credit,
life is one big joke
and we just don't get it.
Kick it into touch!

HEATON: I don't want to wish my life away

on x-box games and virtual play.
I don't want to wake up some guy's "ho"
and end up screaming on the Jeremy Kyle show.
Constantly broke,
and no phone credit,
life is one big joke
and I just don't get it.
I need to kick it into touch!

CHORUS: Constantly broke,
up to our necks in credit,
life is one big joke
and we just don't get it.
We need to Kick it into touch!

SCENE FIVE

Soothill Working Mens' Club.

Parents' meeting.

SPEN: Thanks to parents and family members for coming along. Welcome to Soothill Surfers' Club. We've tried to bring a little taste of the Gold Coast tonight to the "rhubarb triangle".

KIWI PETE: "Batley by the Sea" – now that's asking a lot of climate change.

SPEN: Thank you, Kiwi Pete. We have to wrap up business in time for the bingo at 9.30pm so I'll crack on. Big thanks to everyone who took part in the parents' "touch rugby competition" – even though we finished last.

KIWI PETE: Someone put whiskey in our water bottles.

SPEN: And the "pig racing" was a big success.

KIWI PETE: I heard it was won by a pig this year.

SPEN: Thanks to all those who have made and sold over a thousand designer doggy-poo bags. We are so near, yet so far from our fund-raising target.

If we can't find another five grand by the end of the Summer holidays, we won't be going anywhere. We need one last push, people. The girls are down Tescos every weekend on the tills, packing bags in exchange for donations.

| | We've some fabulous prizes tonight, donated by local businesses: you can win a day out at the assault course at Rothwell, afternoon tea at the local garden centre or a piercing of your own choice at Kick Lane Tattoos. |

KIWI PETE: There y'are, Nan, you'll be able to get the other nipple done.

NAN: I'll swing for you, Kiwi Pete.

SPEN: I've had a new tattoo done for the occasion – and it's itching like hell.

KIWI PETE: Try pile cream. Worked for me.

SPEN: (*showing a rhubarb tattoo on his leg*) The girls have decided on their tour name for the new strip: the "Batley Rhubarbs".

KIWI PETE: The girls want to know when they're getting the new kit?

SPEN: When I get it. I'm sure you'll miss them while they're away and, I'm speaking as a parent now, some of them will be feeling more lonely than others. Obviously pastoral care is down to me. I'm responsible for safety and welfare – it's my coaching badge on the line; but I need your support. I need you to let me know if there's anything I'm not aware of.

KIWI PETE: What's the time difference?

SPEN: They're ahead of us in Oz by nine hours.

KIWI PETE: Three years ahead in the rugby.

SPEN: I appreciate they'll be 10,000 miles away, but what I don't want is parents 'phoning up any time they like.

NAN: What time's lights out?

KIWI PETE: Straight after "Neighbours".

SPEN: I suggest you phone between 9 - 10am, which will be tea-time in Oz. Or you could phone at midnight and help me get them out of bed of a morning.

KIWI PETE: Good luck with our Emley, you'll need it.

SPEN: Right, any questions I'll be at the bar. We've a beer raffle tonight – everyone who buys a ticket for a tenner wins a drink.

At the bar.

KIWI PETE: I hope you'll take good care of my little princess.

SPEN: Your Emley's more than able to take care of herself.

KIWI PETE: This lad, Calder, she's seeing; I don't want him pestering her while she's away.

SPEN: I'll look out for it; boyfriend trouble's the last thing I need.

NAN: Can I have a quiet word, Spen?

SPEN:	'Course.
NAN:	I don't want our Heaton to go.
SPEN:	I told you I'd sort the money.
NAN:	It's not that. Look, thanks for everything you've done; it wouldn't be a problem if it wasn't Australia.
SPEN:	We wouldn't be going, if it wasn't Australia.
NAN:	It's a family matter. We've relatives out there I don't want her to see.
SPEN:	Nan, you can't deny the girl an opportunity of a lifetime?
NAN:	I've already told her.
SPEN:	We need her in the team.
NAN:	I never thought you'd raise the money. I came tonight because I wanted to tell you in person.
SPEN:	She's your grand-daughter, I can't force you; but you're making a big mistake. I'll look after her in Oz; I'll make sure she doesn't get into bother.
NAN:	I'm sorry, I can't allow it. I've got to go.

SCENE SIX

The girls are gathering for training. Calder catches up with Iffy on her way to training.

CALDER: Do you miss me?

IFFY: No.

CALDER: I don't believe you.

Do you remember our first kiss?

IFFY: No.

CALDER: At the swimming baths.

IFFY: It tasted of chlorine.

CALDER: I miss "swimming" with you.

IFFY: You dumped me.

CALDER: You didn't tell me 'bout your dad.

IFFY: He's still my dad.

CALDER: I've changed.

IFFY: I haven't.

CALDER: Come on, I'm cool with it now.

IFFY: That's big of you.

CALDER: I want you.

IFFY: You're loss, not mine.

CALDER: Don't be like that. Forgive and forget.

IFFY: You're with Em.

Calder takes her mobile phone and types in his number.

IFFY: Give that back.

I didn't ask for your number.

CALDER: Text me. You know you want to.

Iffy runs away.

At the training session.

EMLEY: She hangs out on "Greenway" with the older boys.

SHELLEY: How do you know?

EMLEY: Calder told me.

HEATON: Did he used to go out with her?

EMLEY: He says "no".

SHELLEY: Where's she from?

EMLEY: Savile Town. She lives with her aunty.

Iffy arrives. She is wearing pieces of material around her wrists. Spen wants a quiet word. He takes her by the wrists.

SPEN: Not you as well?

IFFY: What?

SPEN: Let me see your arms.

IFFY: Why? What's up?

SPEN:	What are these?
IFFY:	They're prayers.
SPEN:	Take them off.
IFFY:	You think I'm cutting up?

She takes them off and shows him.

	Satisfied? I'm not like Heaton, okay?
SPEN:	Sorry, Iffy, no offence.
IFFY:	None taken. I know you're looking out for us. The prayers help keep me safe.
SPEN:	Didn't see your folks at the Parents' Night?
IFFY:	My dad really wanted to be there; but he's in prison.
SPEN:	Seriously? I thought your dad owned a furniture business?
IFFY:	He does.
SPEN:	I can't tell when you're telling me the truth and when you're winding me up?
IFFY:	Mum's signed the Consent Form – here.

She hands him the form.

	It's all right, her English is very good.
SPEN:	They've no objections to you going on tour?

IFFY: Dad says he'll pay what you need to reach your target.

SPEN: Yeah, right, it's around five thousand quid.

IFFY: I know.

SPEN: Wow, that's very generous. Tell him to email me his business logo and we'll put it on the new strip. That is, if they let him email from prison?

IFFY: He said give me your bank details and he'll transfer the money –

SPEN: I've heard that before.

IFFY: If you don't want it?

SPEN: I'd really like to meet him; thank him in person.

IFFY: He's not a big rugby fan.

SPEN: But he'll come and watch you play?

IFFY: Let's see how his season goes, shall we?

SPEN: Is this straight up?

IFFY: It's real money, all right. My dad don't fuck about.

SPEN: No strings attached?

IFFY: None.

SPEN: No comeback on us? You know I won't have that.

IFFY: I promise.

SPEN: Why rugby, Iffy?

IFFY: Someone says I can't do a thing for no good reason, I'm gonna do it. I tried boxing, but it wasn't for me. I prefer to go to war as a team, don't you?

SPEN: Do I need to sort out a Prayer Room for you at the hotel?

IFFY: I don't think we'll win by praying, do you?

SPEN: I don't know.

IFFY: I'm not like other Muslim girls. I don't get lifts everywhere; I have a bike. My dad isn't a taxi driver; my mum isn't a housewife. I love Christmas. We have a dog. We have a TV; I watch the News and documentaries. I don't stay at home, cooking and cleaning all day; I'm going to be a Criminologist and marry for love.

SPEN: It can't be easy for you, going against your Muslim upbringing?

IFFY: Listen: I've not turned my back on anything. I'm proud of my culture. You want us to integrate; well, here I am. Just teach me the rugby, coach.

Iffy joins the girls.

GIRLS: Touch and pass, kick some ass,
whatever it takes, they will not pass;
making contact keeps us strong,
touch our hearts and pass it on.

IFFY: We going down Tescos again after?

EMLEY: Maybe.

IFFY: I could take you to the Asian supermarket, if you like?

SHELLEY: We daren't go in there.

IFFY: You'll be all right with me, they're really friendly.

EMLEY: We thought you might take us on Greenway?

IFFY: Who's been talking about me?

EMLEY: Calder says you got suspended from school.

IFFY: Did he? What else did he say?

EMLEY: He says a group of Asian girls organised a trip to the seaside with a group of older lads.

IFFY: If you must know, I typed a letter on school paper and forged the Head's signature. We posted it to our parents, asking them for their permission to go on a school trip and £20 towards costs.

HEATON: Hey, what a great scam.

IFFY:	We'd have got away with it too, if one of the parents hadn't phoned the school for more information.
HEATON:	I told you this girl was cool.
IFFY:	(*to Emley*) Did Calder tell you he was one of the older lads?

Emley doesn't answer. The girls return to training, leaving Iffy on her own. Calder arrives and signals to Iffy to join him.

IFFY:	What you doin' here? You'll get me shot.
CALDER:	Just one date, see how it goes?
IFFY:	No.
CALDER:	Give me one hour, that's all I'm asking.
IFFY:	No.
CALDER:	If it's not right, I'll never bother you again.
IFFY:	Calder, if you're serious, you need to tell Em first.
CALDER:	I will, I'm just waiting for the right moment.
IFFY:	Before we go to Oz.
CALDER:	All right, I'm on it.

SCENE SEVEN

Emley's bedroom.

SHELLEY: Why do they call your dad "Kiwi Pete"?

EMLEY: Pete Black – the "All-Blacks". It's Dewsbury logic.

SHELLEY: Oh, I get it. Funny you being called Emley "Black".

EMLEY: Why?

SHELLEY: You know? The way you've been with Iffy.

EMLEY: That's not about race; it's about Calder.

SHELLEY: Whatever you say.

EMLEY: He's coming 'round in a bit.

SHELLEY: You didn't say.

EMLEY: He's got something to tell me.

SHELLEY: I'll go when he comes.

EMLEY: You don't have to.

SHELLEY: I think I do.

EMLEY: How come dad lets you stay, why not Calder?

SHELLEY: It's right, we could be up to no good.

EMLEY: That would shut him up.

SHELLEY: Would you go with a girl?

EMLEY: No way.

SHELLEY: Why not?

EMLEY: 'Cause my whole world revolves around boys – and shopping.

SHELLEY: And the team.

EMLEY: Well, yeah, and the team.

SHELLEY: Who are girls, right?

EMLEY: Yes, of course they're girls; it's a girls' team.

Oh my god, would you go with a girl?

SHELLEY: I might.

EMLEY: You dark horse.

SHELLEY: It's not such a big deal nowadays.

EMLEY: Isn't it?

Have you been with a girl?

SHELLEY: Might have.

EMLEY: Have you been with a boy?

SHELLEY: Might have. I don't see why we have to choose.

EMLEY: Woo, get you. Bloody hell. How long have I known you? I had no idea.

SHELLEY: I don't feel the need to broadcast it.

EMLEY: I won't tell a soul, I swear.

What was it like?

SHELLEY: I thought you and Calder - ?

EMLEY: Yeah, 'course. I meant, you know, with a girl?

SHELLEY: Different. You should try it.

EMLEY: Do you fancy me?

SHELLEY: No.

EMLEY: Why? What's the matter with me?

Calder arrives. Shelley leaves.

CALDER: Can we go somewhere?

EMLEY: See a movie?

CALDER: Can't afford it.

EMLEY: We could go to yours?

CALDER: No.

EMLEY: What's a matter with here?

CALDER: Your dad doesn't like me.

EMLEY: Dad lets me have whatever I want. I'm going to ask him if you can start stopping over.

CALDER: Really?

EMLEY: I think it's time he accepted we're a couple.

CALDER: (*leaving*) Call me when you've spoken to him.

EMLEY: What was it you wanted to say?

CALDER: It'll keep.

Calder leaves.

SCENE EIGHT

Heaton is at Nan's house, Emley is at Kiwi Pete's and Shelley is at Spen's.

Heaton's house.

HEATON: You told Spen I'm not going?

NAN: It's for the best. I don't expect you to understand.

HEATON: I don't need your permission. I've got it off mum.

NAN: When have you seen your mum?

HEATON: She comes onto the estate to buy her weed.

NAN: You're in my care, Heaton; she has no rights.

HEATON: She says she wants to go back to Australia, but she can't because of her criminal record.

NAN: We took her away for her own good.

HEATON: I've got a copy of me Birth Certificate for me passport. I know mum was pregnant with me when you dragged her back to Britain.

NAN: She was only a girl herself, she didn't know her own mind.

HEATON: Like me, you mean? Well I'm not letting you ruin my life, like you ruined hers.

NAN: How dare you? You wouldn't have a life if it wasn't for me.

HEATON: What's that supposed to mean?

NAN: You think your mum wanted you?

HEATON: That is so cruel.

NAN: She hasn't been able to look after you, has she?

HEATON: You're the reason she's an alcoholic.

NAN: Your bloody father's the reason, not me.

HEATON: What d'you mean? Who was he? It says "Father Unknown". I have a right to know.

NAN: Why don't you ask her?

SCENE NINE

Spen's house.

SHELLEY: Em's dad spoils her rotten.

SPEN: He can afford to.

SHELLEY: I'm glad you don't spoil me.

SPEN: I can't believe you just said that.

SHELLEY: It's true.

SPEN: Shell, what do you know bout Iffy?

SHELLEY: What do you want to know?

SPEN: Well, who does she live with?

SHELLEY: Her aunty in Savile Town.

SPEN: She told me her mum signed her Consent Form.

SHELLEY: She calls her aunty, "mum".

SPEN: Why, is her mum dead?

SHELLEY: No, her aunty brought her up. Her mum and dad had lots of kids and her aunty didn't have any, so they gave Iffy to her to look after.

SPEN: Keeps it in the family, I suppose.

SHELLEY: Better than Care, like we do.

SPEN: Is her dad in jail?

SHELLEY:	She's never said. Why?
SPEN:	He's sent us a £5000 donation for the tour.
SHELLEY:	Great, you should be happy.
SPEN:	Yeah, I s'pose. I think it's been in the wash.
SHELLEY:	What? The money?
SPEN:	Laundered.
SHELLEY:	Oh, right, dirty money.
SPEN:	Yeah.
SHELLEY:	That's been in the wash? Sorry.
SPEN:	I never know where I am with her.
SHELLEY:	She's all right.
SPEN:	I want to accept it. God knows it's the difference between going and not. But I can't go public with it.
SHELLEY:	It could be anonymous, a donation?
SPEN:	Do you know, you're a very sensible young girl, Shell?
SHELLEY:	Am I?
SPEN:	Must get it off your mum. I was saying to her last night, you never bring us any bother. We're really proud of you.
SHELLEY:	Do you want me to? I can if you like?

SPEN: You're such an innocent. I still think of you as a little girl holding balloons on a string.

SHELLEY: I asked you how many balloons it would take to lift me off my feet.

SPEN: Did you?

SHELLEY: You never gave me an answer.

SCENE TEN

Emley's house.

KIWI PETE: You all right, Princess?

EMLEY: Dad?

KIWI PETE: What're you after?

EMLEY: Nothing.

KIWI PETE: Do you want some money?

EMLEY: It's not money.

KIWI PETE: Do you want a horse?

EMLEY: I never said.

KIWI PETE: Guitar lessons?

EMLEY: No.

KIWI PETE: Playstation?

EMLEY: You bought me one.

KIWI PETE: Motorbike?

EMLEY: No.

KIWI PETE: New carpet for your room?

EMLEY: No.

KIWI PETE: Holiday?

EMLEY: Not yet.

KIWI PETE: New trainers?

EMLEY: No.

KIWI PETE: What then?

EMLEY: Can Calder stay over?

KIWI PETE: No!

EMLEY: Why not? He's 18, I'm 16 now.

KIWI PETE: I'm not discussing it.

EMLEY: Your girlfriend stays over.

KIWI PETE: Er, who's the parent here? Whose house is it?

EMLEY: It's my house as well.

KIWI PETE: No, you live here.

EMLEY: Thanks very much. I have rights.

KIWI PETE: When you pay some rent, then you can have some rights.

EMLEY: I thought you wanted me to stay on at school?

No response.

I'm not trying to be funny, dad, but you're so old.

KIWI PETE: Not that old.

EMLEY: You were born last century. You don't know how kids today think.

KIWI PETE: I was sixteen once.

EMLEY: Things have changed.

KIWI PETE: Growing up doesn't change.

EMLEY: Yes, it does. Dad, I think Calder's going to finish with me.

KIWI PETE: And you think letting him stop over will make him decide to stay with you?

EMLEY: I want you to treat me more grown-up.

KIWI PETE: You want to sleep with him, you mean.

EMLEY: It's not like it would be the first time.

KIWI PETE: What? I can't believe I'm even discussing this with you.

EMLEY: How old were you when mum had me?

KIWI PETE: That's quite enough.

EMLEY: Dad, I'm not your little princess any more.

Emley is joined by Heaton, Shelley and Iffy as the Teenagers; Kiwi Pete is joined by Spen and Nan as the Parents, for "PARENTS VS TEENAGERS".

TEENAGERS: Parents and teenagers
Are like perfect strangers.
Teenagers are going through different stages,
Passing phases, needing praises,
Feeling like they're living in cages,
Taken hostage by hormones

                And parents in beige trousers,
                Forgetting what it was like to be their age,
                Ripping through rites of passage
                At a furious pace,
                Turning pages in the book of life,
                Trying not to do themselves a damage.

PARENTS: Parents and teenagers
Are like perfect strangers.
Parents who bring home the wages
Are flying into rages
Cos the teenagers are not able
To gauge the dangers,
Teenagers always in our faces,
Lying around like wasters,
Hanging out in all the wrong places,
Racing around in car chases,
Battling with neighbours and legal cases,
No manners, no respect, no social graces.

PARENT 1: While you live under my roof, it's my rules.

TEENAGER 1: That's soooo unfair.

PARENT 2: You must think money grows on trees.

TEENAGER 2: I'm telling mum.

PARENT 3: Act your age and not your shoe size.

TEENAGER 3: It wasn't me.

PARENT 4: You're not going out dressed like that.

TEENAGER 4: Whatever.

PARENT 5:	Watch your lip.
TEENAGER 5:	In a minute.
PARENT 6:	Get off that computer.
TEENAGER 6:	I'm bored.
PARENT 7:	In my day.
TEENAGER 7:	Am I bothered?
PARENT 8:	And what time do you call this?
TEENAGER 8:	And your point is?
PARENT 9:	Where do you think you're going?
TEENAGER 9:	Do it yourself.
PARENT 10:	You treat this house like a bloody hotel.
TEENAGER 10:	It was already like that.
PARENT 11:	Watch your language.
TEENAGER 11:	You never let me do anything.
PARENT 12:	Your room is like a bomb-site.
TEENAGER 12:	It's not that bad.
PARENT 13:	Don't use that tone of voice with me.
TEENAGER 13:	She started it.
PARENT 14:	Less of your back-chat.
TEENAGER 14:	It's the fashion.

PARENT 15: What did your last slave die of?

TEENAGER 15: LOL (Laugh Out Loud).

PARENT 16: When did you last have a bath?

TEENAGER 16: ROFL (Rolling On the Floor Laughing).

PARENT 17: I am not a bloody taxi.

TEENAGER 17: OMG (Oh My God).

PARENT 18: Get off that phone.

TEENAGER 18: Why is it always my fault?

PARENT 19: If I had a pound for every time.

TEENAGER 19: Get out of my room.

PARENT 20: Do I look like a bank manager?

TEENAGER 20: I hate you.

PARENT 21: If you're not happy with it, phone child-line.

TEENAGER 21: I'm on the phone.

PARENTS/
TEENAGERS: Parents and teenagers
are like perfect strangers

SCENE ELEVEN

At the training ground

SPEN: Girls, I've got an important announcement. I'm thrilled to say we've had an anonymous donation from a very generous supporter of this club of £5,000.

IFFY: (*to Shelley*) Anonymous?

SHELLEY: Didn't think your dad would appreciate going public.

SPEN: We are living in divisive times. There are some out there who want us to fail – as a team and as a community. There are some who would divide this team, divide this community. But there are some who choose to pull together. I have faith in this community. I have faith in you girls. No girls' team has done it before. They said it couldn't be done. But I know you girls can do it.

GIRLS' CHORUS: They said we couldn't do their work,
They said we shouldn't ride their bikes,
They said we couldn't wear their trousers,
They said we shouldn't be impolite,
They said we couldn't have the vote,
They said we shouldn't fight,
They said we couldn't have equal pay,
They said we shouldn't have equal rights,
They said we couldn't be educated,
They said we shouldn't be taught,

	They said we couldn't make their laws,
	They said we shouldn't play their sports.
SHELLEY:	Well, this girl can.
HEATON:	And this girl can.
EMLEY:	And this girl can.
IFFY:	And this girl can.
SPEN:	Pack your bags, ladies; we're off to see the wizard; we're going to Oz!

INTERVAL.

PART TWO

Queensland, Australia.

SCENE 1

The Gold Coast. On the beach. The girls are training in tops over their swimwear. Hazel arrives.

GIRLS:	Touch and pass, kick some ass, Whatever it takes, they will not pass. Making contact keeps us strong, Touch our hearts and pass it on.
HAZEL:	Figured I'd find you guys on the beach.
SPEN:	The girls can't believe we're actually training by the sea.
HAZEL:	Bit of a culture shock, I suppose.
SPEN:	I don't know how you coped so well coming to England in Winter, playing on frozen pitches?
HAZEL:	We loved it when it snowed. It was an honour to play in the County of Origin, where it all started.
SPEN:	Yeah, but just because you start a thing, doesn't give you the right to stay ahead of the game: Batley might have won the first ever Cup, but look at us now: can't even make the Super League.
HAZEL:	And you started the women's game in the UK.

SPEN: Now we're playing catch-up with you. Good to see you again, Hazel.

They shake hands.

HAZEL: Same goes, Spen. The girls are looking healthy.

The girls hold hands and run into the sea with a "1, 2, 3, charge!"

SPEN: They're a credit to their sex. Look at them, all shapes and sizes – that's "girl power" for you; bollocks to the media images of what girls should be like.

HAZEL: All body-types welcome in rugby.

SPEN: When you see them like that, you can't imagine them smashing into each other, can you?

HAZEL: Our girls are looking forward to the re-match.

SPEN: We've a few games to go, first; see if we can get into our stride by the time we play you again.

HAZEL: Ipswich first up, is it?

SPEN: Any tips?

HAZEL: Watch out for the heat in that part of Queensland.

SPEN: We're expecting to have to defend more than we're used to, while we're here.

HAZEL: They're big, Polynesian girls. And fast. They'll try to stretch you wide, then smash straight through the middle.

Girls return from the sea.

SHELLEY: It's amazin' here!

SPEN: Girls, you remember Coach Hazel from Smiley High School?

HEATON: Aye up, cock.

Hazel looks to Spen for a translation.

SPEN: Figure of speech.

HAZEL: Enjoying the sunshine, girls?

SHELLEY: Like we've died and gone to heaven.

HAZEL: We have two types of weather on the Gold Coast: sunny and glorious.

EMLEY: Perfect.

HAZEL: As long as you stay between the red flags.

HEATON: We're not little children.

HAZEL: Seriously, if the sharks don't get you, the riptide will.

IFFY: Sharks?

HAZEL: (*leaving*) See you up at the school in the morning. The girls want to say hello. And the boys want to get a good look at you.

EMLEY:	Why haven't we tanned?
HEATON:	We've only been here a day, stupid.
EMLEY:	I think I've got stretch marks on my legs.
SPEN:	What? From when you gave birth?
EMLEY:	That's not funny.
IFFY:	It's "chub-rub" that – you wanna lose some weight off them thighs.
HEATON:	You're joking, she's no further through than a crisp.
EMLEY:	It's not my fault the shops are full of goodies.
IFFY:	It's not the shop's fault you eat too much.
SPEN:	Listen up, ladies. Remember, we're making history here. We are the first girls team ever to tour Oz. It's up to us to set the standard for all those who come after us – both on and off the pitch.

Emley is showing Shelley a message on her phone, but directing her comments at Iffy.

EMLEY:	Look, Calder's text "I love you" – that's "l-o-v-e y-o-u" not "l-u-v u"; he's actually spelt it out proper, like it means something. He sent me this great photo.

She shoves her moby into Iffy's face.

> Don't you think we make a great couple?

IFFY: Get out of my face.

EMLEY: All the girls fancy him. But he's mine.

IFFY: You can keep him.

SPEN: I can't wait for that first whistle. Let's get on with what we do best.

SHELLEY: I love it here. I think I've used up a year's worth of smiles in one day.

SCENE TWO

Smiley High State School.

HAZEL: A big, warm welcome to our friends from the UK – the "Batley Rhubarbs". We hope you'll enjoy your stay on the Gold Coast and your tour of Queensland. You made us all welcome when we toured the UK last year and it's an honour to return the compliment. I know you're looking forward to the return leg with Smiley High at the end of your tour. The Batley Rhubarbs are UK Rugby League Champions. Smiley High are State School Champions. It promises to be a big match. I understand the ambition of many of you Rhubarbs is to one day play for your women's national team, the "Lionesses". Well, I have to tell you that one of our girls won a Gold Medal at the last Olympic Games with our national womens' team, the "Jillaroos".

We pride ourselves on our sport, here at Smiley High, because we pride ourselves on our "can do" attitude. "Negative people have a problem for every solution." That's why we're positive people. We don't believe in "under-achievers" at Smiley High. Everyone achieves at something here: "See it and believe it, you can achieve it."

Or, as our Head of Positive Behaviour is fond of saying: "Life's a game – it matters that much".

SHELLEY:	They greet us like long-lost cousins. Everyone's so friendly. They have names like Axel, Asia and Savannah. Their first lesson of the day is swimming – in the outdoor pool. Every kid looks like an athlete. The canteen serves sushi and salad - not a baked bean in sight.
	Second lesson's rugby. The changing rooms are called "dressing sheds". They have square practise shields.
	Third lesson's outdoor gym. When do they do maths?
	The boys wear weird clothes and have longer hair than me. They're a bit loud, but tons nicer than lads back home.
	And the girls have perfect skin. It's unreal. I wonder if they all turn into zombies at night?

Juxstaposed is a scene between Emley on the phone to Calder and Calder on the phone to Iffy.

EMLEY:	Do you miss me?
CALDER:	'Course I do.
EMLEY:	Why don't you phone me then?
CALDER:	You're in Australia.
EMLEY:	You worried about the cost?
CALDER:	No.

EMLEY:	Am I not worth it?
CALDER:	I didn't say that.
EMLEY:	You could text me.
CALDER:	I have text you.
EMLEY:	You should text me everyday.
CALDER:	I never know what time it is there.
EMLEY:	No excuse.

Iffy answers the phone from Calder.

IFFY:	What're you ringing me for?
CALDER:	I miss you.
IFFY:	I don't miss you.
CALDER:	Don't be so cruel. It's the middle of the night. I can't sleep, thinking about you.
IFFY:	I'm busy.
CALDER:	Come on, I know it's morning there. Where are you?
IFFY:	At a school.

Emley on the phone to Calder (continued).

CALDER:	Are you on your own?
EMLEY:	Why?

CALDER:	No reason. Just wondering if the rest of the girls are with you?
EMLEY:	What're you asking about "her" for?
CALDER:	Who?
EMLEY:	You know "who".
CALDER:	I'm not.
EMLEY:	Do you know what, I'm sick of the sound of your voice.

Calder on the phone to Iffy (continued).

CALDER:	Has Em said owt about us?
IFFY:	What's to say? Look, you need to tell her.
CALDER:	I don't want to hurt her feelings.
IFFY:	Don't be such a coward.
CALDER:	I think she thinks it's over.
IFFY:	Stop trying to be emotionally intelligent, it doesn't suit you – you're male.
CALDER:	I can't live without you.
IFFY:	You'll survive.
CALDER:	I've always loved you.
IFFY:	Stop it now.
CALDER:	Your voice is like treacle pudding.

IFFY: And I suppose you're the custard?

Emley and Iffy both hang up.

SHELLEY: No one stops me wandering off the school field. I go for a walk around the grounds. There's lilac blossom on the trees and bats the size of crows sleeping upside down in the cool of the palms. They don't have pigeons, they have these big Ibis birds with, like, scythes for beaks. I find a complete snakeskin at the side of the road. The snake must have crawled into the hedge and shedded its entire skin. I'm amazed it can just leave its old self behind and start again with a new one, like it's re-inventing itself with a brand new identity. I meet someone called Charlie, with a red car – a convertible. It's our secret.

I'd better get back; they'll be missing me.

Shelley returns to the group. Emley and Iffy turn away from each other.

IFFY: Where you been?

SHELLEY: Nowhere.

What's going on with you and Em?

IFFY: She thinks I'm trying to steal her boyfriend.

SHELLEY: Are you?

IFFY: It's not my fault he keeps texting me.

SHELLEY: You don't have to reply.

IFFY: He's my mate. I've known him longer than her.

SHELLEY: She's jealous, you can't blame her.

IFFY: One minute she's not bothered about him, the next she's all possessive. She blames me for encouraging him.

SHELLEY: He's playing you both, can't you see?

Iffy turns away and Emley turns back to Shelley.

SHELLEY: You should dump him.

EMLEY: Why should I? He's not dumped me.

SHELLEY: He's no good for you.

EMLEY: We are the perfect couple.

SHELLEY: In looks, maybe; but that's all.

EMLEY: Are you saying I'm stupid?

SHELLEY: You're both stupid.

EMLEY: I don't want her to win.

SHELLEY: It's not a competition.

EMLEY: Yes it is.

SCENE THREE

The team arrive at the Ipswich ground.

SHELLEY: Wow, it's a proper stadium.

SPEN: Respect.

EMLEY: Is this where we're playing, coach, on a pro' pitch?

SPEN: They're obviously treating us like the champions we are, ladies. Off you go and find the changing rooms.

SONG: "LET'S PLAY!"

CHORUS: Welcome to the Ipswich sports pavillion,
the Brothers and Sisters Stadium,
where one dollar could win you a million,
at life's casino, come on,
Let's play!

Pokies, keno,
bookies, lotto,
sports and gambling
at life's casino.
This is the lucky country,
where you can double your money
in a land of opportunity.

No dramas, no problems,
place your bets here;
we're feeding the pokies
$12 billion a year.
Life's a gift so gamble away,

> pokies people play everyday
> at life's casino, come on,
> Let's play!

The girls prepare for the match.

HEATON: Em, have you got a mirror app on your Ipad?

Emley passes it to Heaton so she can check her appearance.

IFFY: Has anyone got a spare bobble I can use?

Emley turns away from Iffy.

IFFY: Fine. Be like that. Shell?

Shelley lends her a bobble for her hair.

SPEN: (*calling*) Are you decent?

EMLEY: No, but you can come in.

Enter Spen, timidly.

SPEN: Em, what're you doin'?

EMLEY: Painting me nails, coach.

SPEN: It's rugby league, Em, not Strictly Come Dancing.

EMLEY: There might be cameras.

SPEN: There's no such thing as an attractive action shot when your head is half-way up another girl's ass.

CHORUS: Feeling hot-shot?
Fancy a long-shot?

Step inside,
drop your coins in the slot.
Play the field,
these odds it's a steal,
deal or no deal?
Everybody knows that winners have sex appeal.

Live your life to the full,
you could be hit by a train;
it's an adrenalin rush
and you'll never be the same.
Pokies, keno,
bookies, lotto;
sports and gambling
at life's casino.
This is the lucky country,
where you can double your money.
At life's casino, come on
Let's play!

SPEN:	Come on, you're not kids now, some of you could be playing for your country in a couple of years.
HEATON:	Coach, can you help me strap me tits up?
SPEN:	No, I bloody can't; I'm not your mother –
HAZEL:	(*arriving*) Sounds like you could use a feminine touch?
SPEN:	Hazel, you're an angel.

Hazel takes over helping Heaton while Spen turns away.

SPEN: You never said you were coming to watch?

HAZEL: Spy in the camp, Spen. Just doing my job. There you go, Heaton, see if you can put a few eyes out with those bazookas.

Heaton is a little embarrassed and flattered.

SPEN: Thanks, Hazel.

HAZEL: No dramas. Advantages of being a female coach.

SPEN: Next time I'm bringing Shelley's mum. Right, ladies, we need to get out there and warm up. Remember to pace yourselves; this game's all about the heat.

SHELLEY: We'll be fine, Coach; this is what we've trained for.

HEATON: "Come on you Batley!"

Girls leave for the pitch.

SPEN: Have you seen the clubhouse? It's like a casino: bookies, horse-racing, card tables, slot-machines…

HAZEL: How do you think they pay for the facilities?

SPEN: You're big on gambling out here, aren't you?

HAZEL: Are you a betting man, Spen?

SPEN: Not really.

HAZEL: You will be before you leave Oz. What do you think the odds are against Ipswich?

CHORUS: Who's gonna win?
20 free spins,
it gets under your skin
this thing called gambling.
Fancy a flutter,
first game of the tour?
Have yourself a guess at the final score?
How many games will they win out of four?
At life's casino, come on
Let's play!

On the pitch the girls are sussing the opposition.

SHELLEY: Is that them warming up?

EMLEY: No way, they're boys.

IFFY: Men, more like; they're fucking massive.

EMLEY: Who asked you?

HEATON: Not on the pitch, you two.

Spen and Hazel arrive. Spen clocks the opposition.

SPEN: Shit! You need to wear your skull-caps, ladies. And your gum-shields. That's everyone.

Spen looks at Hazel.

HAZEL: What can I say? It's an industrial area.

SPEN:	So is Batley, but we can't grow rhubarb that big.
HAZEL:	Did I mention the Sisters of Ipswich are State Club Champions?
SPEN:	Now you tell us.

Girls take up their positions for the off. The rest of the cast take up full-size practice-shields to represent the Ipswich team and face the girls like a Roman army.

IFFY:	A team full of black girls – awesome.
HEATON:	Look 'em straight in the eye, girls.
SHELLEY:	I don't know, it might be rude in their culture.

In turn, the girls smash into the shields and are knocked to the ground as the shields advance. They keep getting up and trying again.

CHORUS:	Smash! 4-0.
	Come on you Sisters!
	Come on you Rhubarbs!
	You're showing them too much respect.
	They're scared of you.
	They're in front, ref!
	Smash! 8-0.
	Through the middle.
	Hands-off.
	Over the top.
	Out wide.
	Up 'n' under.
	Smash! 12-0.

> Get stuck in.
> Keep at it.
> Play it.
> Kick it.
> Catch it.
> Run with it.
> Smash! 16-0.
> Feed the ball.
> Break them down.
> Breakout.
> Smash! 20-0.
> Move up, move out,
> drop in , drop out,
> in, in, in,
> out, out, out.
> Smash! 24-0.

HEATON: They keep chopping us in half, Coach.

SPEN: You're a Prop Forward, Heaton, it's your job to keep hammering away. Draw players in, create a space for the others to run into.

CHORUS: Smash! 28-0.

SHELLEY: We're used to goin' forward, not defendin'.

CHORUS: Smash! 32-0.

SPEN: What have I told you, ladies? Quick passes and move up.

Whistle blows for a penalty.

IFFY:	Why is it a penalty when we tackle above chest-height?
HAZEL:	It's the Safe Conduct Code.
SPEN:	Thanks. I'll recommend it to the RLF when we get home.

Whistle blows again.

EMLEY:	Ref says we can't pull their shirts, Coach?
CHORUS:	Smash! 36-0.
LOGAN:	Come on you Rhubarbs!
SPEN:	Good man, we could do with the support.
LOGAN:	No bother, mate.
SPEN:	Are you local?
LOGAN:	Beenleigh. Ex-Pat family, Yorkshire originally.
SPEN:	One of us.
LOGAN:	(*shaking hands*) Logan.
SPEN:	Spen. Pleased to meet you. We're playing Beenleigh, game after next.
LOGAN:	I know.
SHELLEY:	They're tacklin' in pairs, Coach.
SPEN:	Do the same! (*to Hazel*) What's the matter with them? We've done all this in training.

CHORUS: Smash! 40-0.

LOGAN: Bit like watching Batley play Leeds Rhinos, eh?

SPEN: They're so strong.

HAZEL: That's the Polynesians for you.

SPEN: What's their secret?

HAZEL: They say it's a love of root vegetables - taro for the Maoris, cassava for the Fijians; the Tongans and Samoans are just strong, whatever they eat.

LOGAN: You think these girls are big; you should try playing against their fathers.

CHORUS: Smash! 44-0.

HAZEL: They start them off from knee-high to a crocodile.

IFFY: I don't care if we're losing, I love it here: it's not a white-people sport. Imagine a British Muslim girl, from the time she could walk, given a rugby ball and told to run. Imagine a team of them from Batley and Dewsbury, fed potatoes for the next fourteen years and growing up into big women. Imagine a marauding gang of these Muslim girls, in glorious flight, charging down the middle, in full burka and nicab, smashing all before them. One day, sisters, we will be the Polynesians of the rhubarb triangle!

Iffy charges at the shields.

CHORUS: Smash! 48-0.

Whistle blows for end of the match. The girls limp off the pitch.

EMLEY: Aargh, Coach, I've been kicked in the Ossett.

CHORUS: Another win for the bookies –
now who would have thought that?
The players all gather
at the end of the match.
No bad feelings exist
as the teams swop photos and gifts.
A quick post-mortem on the performance
and all bets are off for the rest of the tournament.

SPEN: I want smiles in defeat, girls!

SHELLEY: First time we've never scored in a match.

SPEN: We were out-muscled and out-played.

HEATON: They battered us.

SPEN: I can't teach you what you've learned here today.

HAZEL: "Experience is what you get when you don't get what you want."

SHELLEY: Has she got a saying for everything?

Logan comes to see the team. Heaton thinks she recognises him.

LOGAN:	No shame, girls. They're a warrior people. Rugby is a way of life – for males and females. From an early age, siblings are taught to battle with each other to toughen them up.
EMLEY:	Can we just go shopping tomorrow, Coach?
LOGAN:	Is that our young Heaton?
HEATON:	Uncle Logan!
SPEN:	Oh shit, he's "that" Logan.
HEATON:	You came.
LOGAN:	Wouldn't miss it for the world.
HEATON:	Everybody, this is my Uncle Logan.
SHELLEY:	Seriously? I thought she made him up.
HEATON:	Logan's me mam's, er –
LOGAN:	Cousin.
SHELLEY:	You don't sound very Yorkshire?
LOGAN:	Second generation.
IFFY:	Did you watch the game?
LOGAN:	It was a close call.
IFFY:	48 – Nil?
LOGAN:	I've seen teams do a lot worse against those girls.

SPEN: That's what happens when you don't play as a team, ladies – you know who I mean.

Iffy and Emley look at each other.

EMLEY: Well, excuse us, Coach, while we synchronise our periods.

LOGAN: It's a real achievement coming out here, representing your country.

SHELLEY: Doesn't feel like it at the moment.

IFFY: I want to play them again; I reckon we could do a lot better next time.

HEATON: Can we spend some time together?

SPEN: Sorry, ladies, the coach is waiting.

HEATON: Will you come to the next match?

LOGAN: If it's all right with Coach, I'd like to treat you girls to a trip to Australia Zoo.

Girls cheer.

SPEN: I don't know if that's such a good idea.

Girls complain.

LOGAN: The Zoo's next to the Beerwah ground. The girls could relax for a while before the match?

Girls plead.

SPEN: Okay, okay. Zoo in the morning, match in the afternoon.

SHELLEY: All the way back to the hotel, I can hear the kookaburras in the trees laughing at us.

SCENE FOUR

Shopping centre. Emley catches up with Shelley. She is loaded up with bags. Shelley is on her mobile phone.

EMLEY: I can't tell you how great it is to be shopping again; and in a totally different country; I found the NRL shop, I've bought some amazing tops; and Pandora's, half-price; here, look, I got this little koala; what you got? Who you talkin' to?

SHELLEY: Someone.

EMLEY: Who?

SHELLEY: Just someone I met.

EMLEY: Where? Let me have a look?

SHELLEY: No.

EMLEY: You're on a dating site?

SHELLEY: And?

EMLEY: It'll be full of creeps.

SHELLEY: Charlie's not like that.

EMLEY: Really? Boys from Oz are different, are they?

SHELLEY: I wouldn't know.

EMLEY: Come on. They're all "fuck-boys" like back home; that's all they're interested in. Tell me you've not agreed to meet?

SHELLEY:	None of your business.
EMLEY:	Yes, my business, I'm your mate.
SHELLEY:	Then you should be on my side.
EMLEY:	What's your dad gonna say?
SHELLEY:	Nobody's gonna find out – unless you tell them? I'm sure I can find you a mate, if you wanna come?
EMLEY:	With a complete stranger, Shell? Really? It's dangerous.
SHELLEY:	I'm not stupid. We met at Smiley High.
EMLEY:	I never saw you! How old?
SHELLEY:	Twenty-five.
EMLEY:	Twenty-five! What're you playin' at?
SHELLEY:	It's just a holiday romance.
EMLEY:	You can't meet up again.
SHELLEY:	You're not my dad. You're just jealous.
EMLEY:	Well, if that's what you think…

Emley storms off in disgust.

SCENE FIVE

SPEN: Right, you lot, "Kangaroo Court".

SHELLEY: Awe, do we have to?

SPEN: Yes, we have to. You know the drill.

They set up a "dock" for the accused and a seat for the judge.

HEATON: Who's on trial?

SPEN: Em –

EMLEY: Me? What've I done?

SPEN: And Iffy.

IFFY: What for?

SPEN: Get in the dock, the pair of you. Shelley, you're the Judge today.

They take up their positions.

HEATON: What about me?

SPEN: Star Witness.

HEATON: Cool.

SPEN: (*passing a note to Shelley*) These are the charges, Judge, if you can read them out.

SHELLEY: (*reading*) Emley and Iffy, you stand accused of allowing "boyfriend trouble" off-the-pitch to affect your game on-the-pitch against the Sisters of Ipswich. How do you plead?

EMLEY: (*to Shelley*) What you been saying?

SHELLEY: I haven't said anything. I swear.

SPEN: Answer the charges, ladies.

IFFY: Not Guilty.

SHELLEY: Not Guilty, "Your Honour".

IFFY/EMLEY: Not Guilty, Your Honour.

SPEN: Call the Star Witness.

Heaton takes up her position.

Spen whispers instructions into Shelley's ear.

SHELLEY: Star Witness, can you tell the Court if, in the changing rooms before the match, Emley lent you her Ipad mirror so you could see to brush your hair?

HEATON: Yes, Your Honour. We all like to look our best before a big game because we come off looking like shit.

SHELLEY: And did you hear Iffy ask Emley for a bobble for her hair?

HEATON: Yes, Your Honour.

IFFY: I asked everyone.

SHELLEY: And what was Emley's response to the request?

HEATON: She blanked her.

SHELLEY: Why do you think she blanked her?

HEATON: Dunno, they've been arguing about Calder for ages; it's getting on everyone's nerves.

EMLEY: Hey, that's not fair!

SHELLEY: In your opinion, did this affect our performance against the Sisters of Ipswich?

EMLEY: Watch it, Shell, I could easy ditch the dirt on you, remember?

SHELLEY: Silence in Court! I'll have you for Contempt.

HEATON: Well, now you mention it.

IFFY: Heaton! We were all pussies against the Sisters.

SPEN: Verdicts, Judge?

Spen whispers again into Shelley's ear.

SHELLEY: Guilty, as charged. Both of you.

SPEN: Sentences, Judge?

HEATON: I've got an idea.

Heaton, Shelley and Spen confer.

SHELLEY: Are you sure?

Heaton nods.

Right, you've got to jump in the pool, fully-clothed.

IFFY: No sweat.

SHELLEY: And your mobies are confiscated until after the next game.

EMLEY: No way!

SPEN: Yes, way. The Court's decided. There's no Appeal. Hand them over.

Emley and Iffy hand Spen their phones.

SPEN: (*to Shelley*) Tell you what, I admire your ability to find a girl's weak point – both on and off the pitch.

EMLEY: (*to Shelley*) Remember, you, what goes around, comes around, like that riptide.

SCENE SIX

At the hotel. Emley is face-timing her dad on her ipad.

EMLEY: Dad?

KIWI PETE: Where's your phone?

EMLEY: It's been confiscated.

KIWI PETE: What? Who by?

EMLEY: It's a long story.

KIWI PETE: I'll get onto Spen.

EMLEY: No, don't cause trouble.

KIWI PETE: Well, buy another phone; I can transfer you the money.

EMLEY: I've got me Ipad. I'll get it back after the next match.

KIWI PETE: I'm not happy.

EMLEY: Neither am I.

KIWI PETE: What's up, peach?

EMLEY: I wanna come home.

KIWI PETE: Has something happened?

EMLEY: No. I'm homesick.

KIWI PETE: Is this about that bloody boyfriend of yours?

EMLEY: It's a mess; I don't know what to do.

KIWI PETE: I told Spen to watch out for him bothering you.

EMLEY: You shouldn't do that; you'll get me thrown off the team.

KIWI PETE: I'm not having you upset; not when you're so far away from us.

Emley sheds a tear.

That's it; I'll buy a ticket for you online. Pack your bags, you're coming home.

EMLEY: No, you're over-reacting again. I can't desert the team, it'll be all right.

KIWI PETE: Are you sure?

EMLEY: I just needed a little cry. I miss having you there for a moan.

KIWI PETE: I know, peach. I miss you moaning at me.

EMLEY: We're going to Australia Zoo.

KIWI PETE: Send me photos.

SCENE SEVEN

At Australia zoo, the girls are having their photos taken with the animals.

EMLEY: This is me with a koala.

SHELLEY: This is me with an Emu.

IFFY: This is me with a crocodile.

HEATON: This is me with Uncle Logan. And a kangaroo.

LOGAN: There's no tastier meat than 'roo meat.

HEATON: Urgh!

LOGAN: It's true.

HEATON: But they're so cute and cuddly, how can they do that?

LOGAN: 'Roos are considered pests in the Bush. You're allowed to cull them if they threaten your crops.

HEATON: How can a kangaroo threaten anybody?

LOGAN: You wouldn't say that if you were faced with a mob of roos. They live in groups of ten or more.

HEATON: That's not a "mob", that's a family.

LOGAN: Not sure what that means, Heaton. Long time since we were a family.

HEATON: What happened to us?

LOGAN: How much don't you know?

HEATON: Are you my dad?

LOGAN: Hell, no. Who's told you that?

HEATON: There's no name on my Birth Certificate; Nan said to keep away from you; I thought – sorry; shit, I'm embarrassed.

LOGAN: Look, Heaton, if I was your dad I'd want the world to know how proud I was of you.

SPEN: Right, ladies, we've got ourselves something to prove today. Now, you can get the crap kicked out of you again or you can give it to them this time while getting the crap kicked out of you – which is it to be?

At the match.

CHORUS: Beerwah Bulldogs Stadium,
in the valleys of green and gold;
against the All-Stars of the Sunshine Coast
the next game unfolds.
The All-Stars score first,
but Batley are on a roll:
Heaton wrestles and breaks away,
Iffy kicks to Emley, it's still in play;
the defensive line are foiled
as she swings it out to Shelley and touchdown!
Batley's first try on Ozzie soil.

20-16 to the All-Stars, Final Score,
but the Rhubarbs have finally made their mark, for sure;
a force to be reckoned with, sport;
who knows what's in store?
Watch out Beenleigh,
prepare for some "shock 'n' awe".

SCENE EIGHT

Back at the hotel.

SPEN: Well done, ladies; that was a county team you played today – a bit like us playing Yorkshire – and it was a close call. Main thing is we got on the score sheet. I'm proud of yous.

EMLEY: Thanks, Coach. Can we have our mobies back now?

SPEN: I've left them in your rooms. I suggest you all go for a post-match swim, keep those muscles toned.

Emley and Iffy go to their respective rooms to find their mobiles.

EMLEY: Hang on a minute, this isn't mine.

IFFY: Shit, this is Em's moby.

EMLEY: (*checking Iffy's messages*) I know I shouldn't, but –

IFFY: (*checking Emley's messages*) I wonder what Calder's been saying to her?

On screen appears a text from Calder to Iffy.

EMLEY: (*reading*) "I want us to be "mates" like on the Discovery Channel."

On screen appears a text from Calder to Emley.

IFFY: (*reading*) "You're the only one for me."

IFFY/EMLEY: The two-faced little shit.

Elsewhere in the hotel.

SPEN: Shell's missing.

HAZEL: Are you sure?

SPEN: She's not in her room, she's not in the pool, she's not in the cafe. None of the girls have seen her since they got back from the match.

Emley overhears them as she goes to Iffy's room.

EMLEY: I think I know where she is.

SPEN: Where?

EMLEY: I'm sorry, Spen; she's gone to meet Charlie.

SPEN: Who the fuck's Charlie?

EMLEY: Someone she's met.

SPEN: You knew about this?

EMLEY: I told her not to go.

SPEN: You don't tell her, you tell me!

HAZEL: Calm down, Spen, she's telling you now.

SPEN: Yeah, when it's too late. Where's she meeting him?

EMLEY: I don't know.

SPEN: Who is he?

EMLEY: I've not met him.

SPEN:	How old is he?
EMLEY:	Twenty-five.
SPEN:	Twenty-five! What-the-fuck! How did she meet him?
EMLEY:	Online.
SPEN:	Oh that's just great!
HAZEL:	(*leaving*) I'll call the police.
SPEN:	She's only just turned sixteen and she's gone AWOL with a twenty-five year old pervert. We're 10,000 miles away from home and her mum'll be ringing me at any minute. (*to Emley*) Look, this is serious; what else do you know about him?
EMLEY:	He drives a red car. It's a convertible, that's all I know.
SPEN:	She could be anywhere by now. Anything could have happened.
HAZEL:	(*returning with the other girls*) They're on their way.
SPEN:	We have to look for her. You stay here for the police. I'll go to the shopping centre. Girls, go to the beach – take your phones.

Shelley returns, unaware of the chaos. Spen runs to hug her.

SPEN:	Come here! Has he hurt you? I'll kill him!

SHELLEY:	I'm all right, dad. What's the panic?
SPEN:	Where the fuck have you been?
SHELLEY:	For a walk on the beach.
SPEN:	Don't lie to me! We know you were meeting him. The police are out looking for you.
SHELLEY:	What? I decided not to go.
SPEN:	Are you telling me the truth?
SHELLEY:	Yes, I swear down.

Spen falls to his knees. Hazel consoles him.

SHELLEY:	I'm sorry, dad; I didn't mean -
HAZEL:	Go to your rooms, girls.
SHELLEY:	I'm not a child!
SPEN:	You're acting like one, in front of Hazel.
HAZEL:	It's all right, Spen.
SHELLEY:	Grow up, will you!
SPEN:	Me, grow up? That's rich coming from you, young madam.
SHELLEY:	You don't know anything about me!
SPEN:	I'm not sure I want to know.

Shelley and the girls leave.

SPEN: Who, in their right mind, would take on looking after a group of young women?

HAZEL: A pimp?

Emley and iffy meet to swap phones.

EMLEY: I didn't... did you?

Iffy shakes her head.

EMLEY: I might have just... by mistake.

IFFY: Me too.

They acknowledge they have both read each other's messages.

IFFY: Nothing's happened, I swear.

EMLEY: I know.

IFFY: If he behaves like that with you, he'd be the same with me, or anyone.

EMLEY: I was thinking, maybe we should teach Calder a lesson?

IFFY: Let's hatch a plan...

SCENE NINE

On the coach to Beenleigh.

SPEN: What're we up against today, Hazel?

HAZEL: Bit of a mixed bunch, really. Lots of migrant families: Brazilian Africans, Philipinos and, of course, Polynesians. And the "Murri Sisters" – aboriginal girls.

SPEN: This is one hell of a country.

HAZEL: A lot of the girls come from the government housing estate on the edge of town –

SPEN: Like our council estates?

HAZEL: Some of them take up rugby to avoid the drugs and teenage pregnancy.

SPEN: Not so different then to Batley.

HAZEL: The school has its own farm. They rear "droughtmaster" cattle and sell their produce to the local abattoir, where many of the local kids end up working.

SPEN: Sounds like I'd better go and psyche 'em up for the match.

Spen turns to the girls.

Iffy and Emley are laughing and joking together.

SHELLEY: You two seem very matey today?

EMLEY: What do you mean? Me and Iffy are best mates, aren't we?

IFFY: Got loads in common, we have.

SHELLEY: Like Calder, you mean?

EMLEY: Like girly revenge on that douche-bag.

SHELLEY: What have you two done?

IFFY: Nothing. Just shared our feelings with the world.

EMLEY: We posted all his texts to both of us on Facebook.

IFFY: So everybody can see what a two-faced little player he is.

SHELLEY: Yeay, girl power; I'm loving it.

Heaton has her head down, listening to music.

SPEN: What's up, Heaton?

HEATON: Nothing. I'm listening to "angry" music to get me in the mood for the match.

SHELLEY: Show us your angry face, Heaton?

Heaton obliges and they fall about laughing.

SPEN: Come on, ladies, let's lift those spirits: Team Song, everyone. Heaton, why don't you lead the charge?

Call and response chant.

HEATON: Everywhere we go-o,

CHORUS: Everywhere we go-o,

HEATON: People want to know-o,

CHORUS: People want to know-o,

HEATON: Who we are?

CHORUS: Who we are?

HEATON: Where we come from?

CHORUS: Where we come from?

HEATON: Shall we tell them?

CHORUS: Shall we tell them?

HEATON: We're the Batley,

CHORUS: We're the Batley,

HEATON: The Batley Batley Rhubarbs,

CHORUS: Batley Batley Rhubarbs...

HEATON/ CHORUS: B-A-T-L-E-Y, B-A-T-L-E-Y BATLEY!

At the match.

CHORUS: Batley versus Beenleigh:
two teams, evenly matched,
two towns, both with changing identities.

BEENLEIGH CHORUS: Beenleigh: on the Logan and Albert Rivers;
Brisbane overspill into agricultural lands –
traditionally sugar cane and rum distilleries;
taken over by new industries.

CHORUS: Batley: Danish settlement,
near the River Calder,
mentioned in the Doomsday Book;
up on its history, down on its luck;
coal mines and mills given over to retail.
First try goes to Batley: 4-Nil.

BEENLEIGH: Early German and Anglo-Saxon settlers
are joined by the latest migrant labour;
in good Lutheran tradition,
we're all foreigners here.
Second try to Beenleigh: score 4-4.

CHORUS: 60% of under 18's in Batley
are now of South Asian origin,
so what do we mean any more by "foreign"?

BEENLEIGH: Something you Brits don't have
is an indigenous black population;
but slowly we are "Closing The Gap",
respecting the rights of the native peoples -
the "Custodians of the Land".
That's another try for the home side
and the score stands at 8-4 to Beenleigh.

CHORUS: It's true that Life Expectancy is lower in Batley;
there's binge-drinking, drugs and obesity,

	unemployment and anxiety,
	depression and poverty,
	increasing levels of crime –
BEENLEIGH:	And problems with dentistry –
	What? That's why we smile more in Oz -
CHORUS:	Yes, of course, because of the climate, we know,
	and yet, still we try –
	8-8.
BEENLEIGH:	We have our own problems with racism, same as you guys.
CHORUS:	And try again –
	12-8.
BEENLEIGH:	And home-grown terrorism.
CHORUS:	Until, finally, against all the odds,
	14-8,
	we achieve our first, historic victory.

Heaton comes off the pitch, carrying the ball. Logan congratulates her with a hug.

LOGAN:	Top banana! You were amazing.
HEATON:	Thanks; I'm really glad you came.
LOGAN:	Great game.
HEATON:	We need to talk.
LOGAN:	Not now.

HEATON: Yes now.

LOGAN: Not here.

HEATON: Yes here.

The others leave them alone.

LOGAN: It's not exactly my place to tell you.

HEATON: Well, no other bastard seems willing to.

LOGAN: It's like this: your Nan and Grandad came over to live in Queensland to be near your Grandad's brother and his wife – my mum and dad.

HEATON: Mum was a teenager, wasn't she?

LOGAN: Yeah. Me and your mum, we were cousins. We got on fine, she was a good kid.

HEATON: So what happened?

LOGAN: Your Nan hated it here, your Grandad loved it; your mum copped for a whole lot of bickering so she used to spend a lot of time at my folks'.

HEATON: With you?

LOGAN: I left home, working away for a while. When your mum fell pregnant at 16, your Nan took her back to the UK.

HEATON: So why the big secret? Who was my dad?

LOGAN: Heaton, my folks are both dead now.

HEATON:	Who?
LOGAN:	Mum told me before she died.
HEATON:	Who?
LOGAN:	My dad was also your dad.
HEATON:	That's disgusting.

Heaton runs away.

REPRISE OF "KICK IT INTO TOUCH"

HEATON: What have I done to deserve all this?
Where did I go wrong?
Who am I really?
And where do I belong?
Lied to by my folks,
I was born to regret it,
my family's one big joke
and I just don't get it.
Kick it into touch!
I'm sick of all the lies,
I don't care about their remorse,
I don't want to be a part of this family,
I don't want to play rugby no more.
Lied to by my folks,
I was born to regret it,
my family's one big joke
and I just don't get it.
Kick it into touch!

She puts down the ball and leaves.

SCENE TEN

At the hotel. Spen and Shelley are in one room, Heaton and Uncle Logan in another.

SPEN:	You said, "I don't know anything about you"; so I'm here to find out.
SHELLEY:	That doesn't exactly sound like someone who's willing to listen.
SPEN:	I can't do right for doing wrong.
SHELLEY:	I know your heart's in the right place, dad.
SPEN:	Am I paying too much attention to the other girls, is that it?
SHELLEY:	I do get a bit jealous, that's true.
SPEN:	I have to be seen to treat you all the same.
SHELLEY:	I know. And you do. That's not it.
SPEN:	I started this team for you.
SHELLEY:	You started it for yourself.
SPEN:	That's harsh.
SHELLEY:	I need to feel special. Not on the pitch. Off the pitch.
SPEN:	Is that why you scared the shit out of me?
SHELLEY:	Maybe. I'm trying to tell you something.

In Heaton's room.

LOGAN: Coach tells me you don't want to play?

HEATON: How can you accept what they've done to us?

LOGAN: What choice do we have? We need to move on.

HEATON: No wonder mum's so fucked up.

LOGAN: They had an affair. What he did was very wrong. She was only sixteen.

HEATON: She knew what she was doing. It's your mum I feel sorry for.

LOGAN: I'm sorry for your trouble.

HEATON: You realise, this means we're…

LOGAN: Yeah, I know, I'm your bro'. Scary thought, isn't it?

HEATON: I can hardly think it, let alone say it.

LOGAN: I must admit, I prefer "uncle", given the age gap and all.

Back in Shelley's room.

SHELLEY: I don't know if you've noticed, but I'm an incurable romantic?

SPEN: Like me.

SHELLEY: You're a sentimental old cynic.

SPEN: Less of the old.

SHELLEY:	I love playing rugby, but I also love stuff like poetry.
SPEN:	You can do both.
SHELLEY:	I do.
SPEN:	I'd like to read some of your poetry, if you don't mind?
SHELLEY:	Really?
SPEN:	I'm not a complete philistine. Look, you might be romantic but men will exploit that for sex.
SHELLEY:	Charlie's not a man.
SPEN:	What're you telling me? Em said it was a "he".
SHELLEY:	I never said that; she must've assumed.
SPEN:	So you're gay now, all of a sudden? Listen to yourself.
SHELLEY:	No, you listen to yourself. It's the stereotype, I know; but if 10% of women are gay, some of them will be rugby players. That goes for the men too.
SPEN:	10%?
SHELLEY:	We're on the "up" – so to speak.
SPEN:	Does your mother know?
SHELLEY:	Yeah. Well, she suspects, anyway.

SPEN: Am I always the last to be told? So you did meet up with this "Charlie" woman?

SHELLEY: Yes. I'm not sorry, it was fun.

SPEN: You lied to me.

SHELLEY: I am sorry for that. I'm still holding those balloons, dad. But this time I feel like I'm being lifted up into the air and floating across the sky.

SPEN: (*leaving*) You're absolutely right: I have no idea who you are.

SHELLEY: I can't believe I've just "come out" to me dad.

Back in Heaton's room.

HEATON: I don't know what to do now?

LOGAN: You could come and live in Oz? Seriously, I could get you into one of the rugby schools.

HEATON: I've given up on rugby.

LOGAN: You mustn't, you're a top player; I've seen you in action.

HEATON: I'm not good enough to play here.

LOGAN: You soon would be. You'd flourish at Smiley High.

HEATON: How could I live here?

LOGAN: I'd look after you.

HEATON: You'd do that for me?

LOGAN: Damn right I would, after everything that's happened.

HEATON: I don't know if I could ever leave me Nan.

LOGAN: The Gold Coast is one of the Top Ten happiest places on the planet to live.

HEATON: Then why are we so unhappy?

SCENE ELEVEN

Smiley High State School. The girls are on the pitch, warming up for the game, except for Heaton. Spen and Hazel are on the touchlines.

SPEN: I can't believe the facilities you've got at this school.

HAZEL: Yeah, well, we don't sell off our sports fields to property developers, like you guys in the UK.

SPEN: How many girls do you have wanting to play rugby?

HAZEL: There's 85 want to get involved – 18 are selected.

SPEN: That's amazing.

HAZEL: Believe me, we might be State High School Champions, but it's still a battle with the authorities to keep the programme going.

SPEN: You love your sports more in Oz. There's more respect.

HAZEL: We appreciate "The Great Outdoors" – life's a good barbeque.

SPEN: We treat "The Great Outdoors" as a problem.

HAZEL: On the other hand, it's an eleven-hour drive out West to see my son.

SPEN: Your girls aren't wandering around the streets or hanging around pubs, like ours.

HAZEL: Yeah, but when our girls toured the UK, they went AWOL on me. I had to wait up half the night 'cause they'd been out clubbing.

SPEN: It's hard to keep them focused on their training.

HAZEL: I'm sure your girls will be up for it today: after all, this is your "revenge" match.

SPEN: I like to think it's more good-natured than that. Don't get me wrong, we want to beat you, all right; but we have to be realistic. We've come here to learn.

HAZEL: Bollocks, Spen, you've come here to win.

SPEN: Not at any cost.

HAZEL: You see, that's why we're better at winning.

SPEN: "At any cost" leads to corruption and sports people taking banned drugs and the like.

HAZEL: I don't agree with drugs. I'd have a life ban for everyone using drugs.

SPEN: I'm starting to wonder how many champions will be left, if we do that?

HAZEL: There will always be champions. Sports are about winning.

SPEN: It has to be more than that, doesn't it?

HAZEL: Not in my book.

Logan turns up with Heaton. Spen signals his gratitude to Logan and takes Heaton to one side.

SPEN: Good to have you back. Let me see your arms.

Heaton shows him. They have fresh marks.

I know it's not going to be easy, lass, but we're here for you; this is your rugby family.

HEATON: Thanks, Coach.

Heaton joins the girls.

Girls position themselves and the game starts.

SPEN: Good to see a female referee.

HAZEL: Times like this, I really miss playing.

SPEN: Don't we all? I miss the banter. You were a "jillaroo", weren't you, Hazel?

HAZEL: 2008 Runners-Up in the World Cup, at the Sunscorp Stadium, Brisbane. Lost to New Zealand in the final 34-0.

SPEN: No shame there.

HAZEL: No; but like I tell our girls every week: if you think training's hard, try losing a World Cup Final.

SPEN: I hope I can be a better coach than I was a player. I grew up in a working-class household, the only boy among three sisters.

I knew my sisters were more athletic than me, but I was the only one allowed to go professional. I know I'm part of making changes for these girls; that's enough for me.

HAZEL: How's it going with your Shelley?

SPEN: I think I might have failed her as a dad.

HAZEL: At least she's agreed to play.

Heaton runs off the pitch, holding her chest.

HEATON: Coach, I'm in trouble.

SPEN: What's happened? Are you hurt?

HEATON: (*whipping off her bra*) Me bra strap's snapped.

SPEN: Give me that! What have I told you about wearing a training bra?

HEATON: Have you got a spare one?

SPEN: No, I bloody well haven't. What do you think I am – a mobile lingerie shop?

HEATON: What am I gonna do?

SPEN: I don't know, do I?

HEATON: I can't play without one.

HAZEL: Here, she can have mine.

Hazel whips off her bra and shields Heaton, so she can put it on.

HEATON: Thanks, Coach.

HAZEL:	No dramas. I think you'd best hang on to it.
SPEN:	No wonder we're bloody losing.
HAZEL:	You don't get that in the men's game.
CHORUS:	Real tough game for one and all, Smiley High swing down like a wrecking ball; but Batley keep rolling it back up the hill in what quickly develops into a battle of wills. Despite a late try from Batley, final score: 14-4 to Smiley High. Life's never like it is in the movies.

Players leave the pitch. Spen and Hazel swap gifts after the match.

Grown-ups form one group and girls the other, for a reprise of "PARENTS VS TEENAGERS"

CHORUS:	Parents and teenagers are like perfect strangers until it comes to the rugby: it's like your second family. Learning how to listen to grown-ups, facing the unknown; seeing your kids deal with pain, getting hurt and bouncing back again; learning right from wrong, feeling safe and strong, honour and decency, loyalty to your team-mates, celebrating success and enjoying the game, appreciating your own body and your own beauty,

the difference between female and feminine,
discipline and self-discipline;
knowing how to fail,
how to make mistakes and recover,
shaking hands when it's all over,
forgive and forget, get on with it
and respect for the opposition.
Parents and teenagers
are like perfect strangers
until it comes to the rugby,
it's like your second family.

END.